Praise and Worship You

By

Rod Loader

INTRODUCTION

I stood among many others, closed my eyes and raised my hands. In those minutes, while my lips sang the words, my heart and mind felt like they were in God's amazing presence. I yearned for nothing more. I understood the true wonder that is Praise and Worship.

Did I have the same experience every time I sang the same songs or sat in the same seat? No. But that's okay. God touched me in those moments. That was time between God & I. A time when He let me know how wonderful and personal Praise and Worship can be.

Have I felt that way again? Yes, during times my heart and soul were focused on Him alone. When I hungered and thirsted for Him. Often this was during church prayer evenings, when the pastor insisted we spend at least thirty minutes personally praising, worshiping and seeking God, before we began corporate prayer. These were the most powerful prayer sessions I have ever attended. All because we started by seeking, praising and worshipping God.

Too often, this world pulls us away from God. We barely have enough time for quick prayers, let alone giving time to praise and worship. Yet, without it we feel flat, uninspired, unable to lift ourselves above the struggles surrounding us. We need the regular touch we get from God when we praise and worship.

With every poem He gave me, I was encouraged to praise and worship Him more and I am always amazed at how awesome and wonderful He is.

He taught me a great deal about Himself and a life with Him as He shared them with me and has given me the desire to share them with you.

I pray you will be as blessed by reading them as I still am.

Rod Loader

Revelation 19:3-7

³And again their voices rang out: "Praise the LORD!
The smoke from that city ascends forever and ever!"

⁴Then the twenty-four elders and the four living beings fell down
and worshiped God, who was sitting on the throne. They cried out,
"Amen! Praise the LORD!"

⁵And from the throne came a voice that said,
"Praise our God, all his servants, all who fear him, from the least to
the greatest."

⁶Then I heard again what sounded like the shout of a vast crowd or
the roar of mighty ocean waves or the crash of loud thunder:
"Praise the LORD! For the Lord our God, the Almighty, reigns.

⁷Let us be glad and rejoice, and let us give honor to him."

FOR THE LORD

Are you willing to sacrifice your life?
Are you willing to give it all tonight?
For the Lord.
I'm not saying to end your life in pain.
I'm just asking to start your life again.
For the Lord.
I'm asking you to come up here with me.
I'm asking you to live a life so free.
For the Lord.

Chorus
It's for the Lord we live.
And for the Lord we try.
It's for the Lord we love.
And with the Lord we fly.
For the Lord.

Will you carry on living for the land.
Or change your mind, by reaching out your hand.
For the Lord.
Let me show you love coming from God's heart.
Come take my hand while giving up your heart.
For the Lord.
Christ changed my life and made me someone new.
He'll change your life if you allow him to.
For the Lord.

Chorus

END

THE PICTURE

Paint me a scene,
In auburn and green.
Frame it with golden sunshine.
Fill it oh please,
With wildlife and trees.
This land I long to be mine.

When it has been done,
Please paint me the Son.
Let him live long in my mind.
Sign it with love,
From God up above.
That I am thankful to find.

END

A NEW MASTER

Oh, I know what it's like to be hungry,
For the gospel of the Lord.
Yes, I know what it's like to be thirsty,
For the water from the Lord.

Yes, I know what it's like to be poorly,
When His blessing I don't have.
Oh, I know what it's like to be lonely,
When I'm searching for his love.

It was Jesus who gave me my freedom,
From the emptiness of sin.
It was Jesus who opened the doorway,
As he stood and called me in.

It was Jesus who made the new person,
Oh, as I was born again.
It is Jesus who is my new Master,
And I now am serving him.

END

FOOT OF THE CROSS

Lord Jesus,
Let me stand,
At the foot of the cross.
Where you died for me,
And you set me free,
So we might gain,
From your suffering and loss.

Lord Jesus,
Come and be,
My new guiding light.
And you'll guide me true,
In the ways of you,
So we will meet,
In the kingdom of light.

END

FEAR

Please let me help, my precious child.
Your heart races, your tears run wild.
Each breath is hard, you feel defiled.
When fear does grip your soul.

How every choice seems hard to make,
And end results keep you awake,
And you can't find a choice to take,
For fear is in control.

But fear, my child, is not from me,
For it comes from your enemy,
Who uses it so you aren't free,
So fear will take its toll.

But I offer sweet love and peace,
To break those bonds and give release,
So your freedom will never cease,
And fear won't grip your soul.

Please trust in me, my precious one,
Just let me lead, my will be done,
And find my peace, through Christ my Son,
Then fear will not control.

Then I will lead and you obey.
My true love casts fears away.
Oh, I'll show you a better way,
Where fear won't take its toll.

END

TAKE ALL OF ME

You gave me the chance to live again.
You gave me your love to hide the pain.
You gave me the Son to chase the rain.
Now come and take all of me.

You opened my heart and took my pride.
You spread out your arms to let me hide.
You sent down your Son until he died.
Now come and take all of me.

END

STORYBOOK HERO

My Lord is like a story book hero,
But He's as real as you and I.
When my life is so down in the valleys,
Then He will lift me up so high.

My Lord is there whenever I need Him,
And He will guide me on my way.
When my load weighs heavy on my shoulders,
He will take it so far away.

Chorus
You're my God, my Master, my Saviour,
You're my King, my Jesus, my Lord.
You're the one I always will cling to,
Till the day you call me home.

My Lord will share in all of my journeys,
All my good times and when I cry.
Without Him near my life would be nothing,
Only with Jesus I will fly.

Chorus
You're my God, my Master, my Saviour,
You're my King, my Jesus, my Lord.
You're the one I always will cling to,
Till the day you call me home.

END

THE SERVICE

When pews are full the music stops.
The preacher takes the stand.
His mind is full of holy words,
A Bible in his hand.

"I've never seen a finer group,
Of people to be born.
In Jesus name I welcome you,
To service this fine morn'.

We'll sing a hymn to start the day,
Let's hear the voices ring.
My favourite is Amazing Grace,
So, guess what we will sing.

So now to share the word of God,
With Bible held so high.
We'll learn of things in Jesus' time,
And why He had to die.

Continued next page…

From Adam's time to Paul in Rome,
The wonders we're to share.
Then when I'm done, we'll praise the Lord,
And go to Him in prayer.

To thank Him for His wondrous gifts,
We'll cherish one more hymn.
Then close in prayer and praising words,
And worship unto Him.

So, thank you all for coming here,
I wish each one could stay.
In Jesus name I pray the best,
As you go on your way.

Then if in love you do come back,
To worship in His name.
With open heart I'll welcome you,
In Jesus precious name."

END

PRECIOUS SIGHT

Oh, when I stood at the foot of the cross,
I saw Your feet that had walked so many miles.
I saw the nails that had pierced Your precious flesh,
And I felt the pain of one too many trials.

As I looked up into Your precious face,
I saw a sight that will fill my every day.
Within Your eyes was a love without an end,
You gave me sight that man can't take away.

END

MY RESTING PLACE

I'm caught between the concrete and the clay,
I wonder why the nighttime fears the day.
I'm lost amongst the memories on the way,
I smile because God's loving me today.

I'm surrounded by such anger and despair,
I feel the heat of hatred in the air.
Oh, Father I would rather be elsewhere,
But your love lets me face the pain out there.

I'm tested by the ones who leave their mark,
I'm left alone to suffer in the dark.
I know their bite is much worse than their bark,
But you, Jesus, give me a guiding spark.

The world is just an onward rushing race,
And it is run at such a hectic pace.
But you, Spirit, helps me to find space,
And I'm glad your love's my resting place.

At last I feel there's somewhere I belong,
My heart is filled with such a wondrous song.
My love for God has grown so very strong,
I now have learnt His love cannot be wrong.

END

DIRECTION FROM ABOVE

I lived my life within the world,
That turned its back on you.
I strove to do the best I could,
Not caring what was true.
I didn't care whom I had hurt,
Or caused to weep in pain.
My only want was to succeed,
In counting out my gain.

But when at last I could succeed,
The world lashed out at me.
The devil drove me to my knees,
And laughed while mocking me.
The hatred boiled within my heart,
But nothing could I do.
I didn't know there was a way,
To get some help from you.

I heard your name as if by chance,
Or maybe it was 'planned'.
I learnt of love you had to share,
And could not understand.
As weeks went by my desperate heart,
Kept coming back to you.
Then finally I had to search,
To find out what was true.

Continued next page…

You saw me fail there in the world,
Where life is cheap and mean.
Where Jesus is a hated word,
And love is rarely seen.
You loved me though I loved you not,
And lived my life in sin.
Though when I opened up my heart,
You thanked me and came in.

I thank you Lord for loving me,
When I had failed life's test.
And giving me a welcome home,
A place to come to rest.
I praise you Lord for giving me,
The chance to live so free.
Though now I weep for all the souls,
That never get set free.

So many more out in the world,
That do not know the peace.
That comes when you go in their hearts,
And cause their sins to cease.
I feel you want me to go out,
To share with them your love.
And let them know I get all my,
Directions from above.

END

<u>NOW AT HOME</u>

When trumpet sounds and Prince appears,
I'll know the time has come.
With evil cast in fiery pits,
I'll know that God has won.

When dead will rise to heavens high,
I'll know the judgements here.
When all is shown in sinner's lives,
I'll know I'll have no fear.

When heavens gates are open wide,
I'll know which way I'll roam.
When God Himself will call me child,
I'll know I've found my home.

END

WALKING WITH THE ANGELS

I am walking with the angels,
I am living life so free.
I haven't got a single care,
'Cause he is here with me.

I'll live my life just for Jesus,
He'll guide my every way.
I'll live a life with joy and peace,
Oh, every night and day.

I'd given up the will to live,
He gave me brand new life.
His love then came and filled my heart,
He took my fear and strife.

All the things that He has taught,
I gladly learnt from Him.
I'm glad He came into my life,
And took my life so grim.

Praise Him now with hallelujahs,
Praise Jesus, Lord of all.
He suffered the crucifixion,
To save us from a fall.

He was at the resurrection,
'Cause He's the one who rose.
He offered us His holy kingdom,
And said, "Come if you choose."

END

A TRULY AWESOME DREAM

I had a dream, a truly awesome dream,
Of a time that may not be far away.
In my dream I was standing in a clearing,
And the people they came from everywhere.
'Till before long there was just a sea of faces,
That stretched as far as the eye could see.

Then a noise rang out that sounded like a trumpet,
And silence filled the mouths of all 'round me.
Then down from Heaven came a multitude of angels,
More than I dreamed I would ever see.
And in the midst was throned the King of Glory,
And His light shone out for all the souls to see.

Then I fell down on my knees as I saw Him, His glory,
And I praised with all my soul, His majesty.
Then I looked around to see what was happening,
And I saw a sight that filled me with such joy.
Everyone I saw had bowed on bended knee,
And was crying out that Jesus Christ is Lord.

END

THE WORLD TO PRAY

If I could teach the world to pray,
This is what they'd say.
"Give me a heart that's open wide,
To all the things you give.
Then let the spirit fill my life,
And teach me how to live.
Then let my God come shining through,
To each and every one.
And let my Lord forever be,
God's one and only Son."

Chorus
If I could teach the world to pray,
I'd reach them one by one.
If we could teach the world to pray,
We could reach everyone.

If I could teach the world to pray,
This is what they'd say.
"Let us see a heaven full,
With angels all around.
An in the middle there would stand,
The wearer of the crown.
And we would see our Father God,
Shining on His throne.
And He would say come children come,
Let Jesus take you home."

Chorus

END

TIMES (JESUS COME AND BE MY FRIEND)

It's the love I've given to other things,
That leaves me bare inside.
It's the times I'd dare not call out your name,
For foolish selfish pride.

It's the times I have spent avoiding you,
That hurts me deep inside.
It's the time I have spent away from you,
That's why my heart has cried.

Chorus
Jesus, Jesus, come and talk to me,
Jesus, Jesus, come and set me free,
Oh, Jesus come and hold my hand,
Oh, my Jesus come and be my friend.

It's the hate I have shown to other men,
That leaves me hard and cold.
It's the lies I have told to hide my shame,
And truth I've bought and sold.

It's the times I have thought I've done it all,
Without you by me side.
And the times I have found by losing out,
From you I cannot hide.

Chorus

It's the times I have finally learnt the truth,
And bowed before your throne.
It's the times you are calling out my name,
I know I'm going home.

Chorus

END

MY PRICELESS CHILD

He just longs,
To touch your hand,
To touch your face,
To let you know,
You won the race.

It's not about,
The good or bad,
The things you've done,
The things you're not,
For they've all gone.

It's who you are,
Right here and now,
He's reaching down,
To take your hand,
To give a crown.

"My priceless child,"
He says, "Here's what,
You mean to me.
I sent my Son,
To set you free."

"The fights not yours,
The war is won,
Sin's history,
Now let my love,
Bring you to me."

END

I'LL SHARE

I never thought I'd be the one,
To write sweet words about God's Son.
To share through verse of Father's love,
And help folks look to God above.

Yet through all this one thing I've learned,
Nothing I've gained, I've truly earned.
It's all from God, through His great grace,
Which keeps my ego in its place.

When time is done and He calls me,
To live with Him eternally,
I pray that I, in all that time,
Will thank Him for these words in rhyme.

But while I'm here of God I'll share,
For Him the most I truly care.
And while He shares through His Spirit,
I'll tell the world that God is it.

END

IF I DON'T WAKE

I may not see the sea washed sand,
When foam topped billows roll.
Or hear the morning rooster cry,
When dawn is fresh and cold.

I may not touch the sweet young shoots,
When fire or drought have passed.
Or smell the stench of smog filled air,
That cities have to gasp.

I may not long for quitting time,
Like workers on the line.
Or sit in thought with pad and ink,
For words to make a rhyme.

For God may call me home to Him,
While I am very young.
Before I've made my mark on life,
Or heard a song by sung.

Don't grieve for me if I am gone,
Don't throw your life away.
For God will hold me in his arms,
And there I know I'll stay.

END

MY PRAISE TO GOD

In the sweetness of the golden bloom,
In the softness of the falling snow.
In the calmness of the soaring bird,
Your majesty shines through.

In the boldness of the thunders roll,
In the vastness of the open sky.
In the freshness of the rising sun,
Your victory is new.

In the bleakness of the dying Christ,
In the brightness of the empty tomb.
In the greatness of the King's return,
Your life for me is new.

END

PRAISE AND WORSHIP YOU

They nailed your hands to the bloodstained cross,
They put your feet in place.
They pierced your brow with a crown of thorns,
But they couldn't take you kingly place.

Chorus
Jesus, Father God, Holy Spirit come and fill me,
Jesus, all I want to do is praise and worship you.

They laid you down in a borrowed tomb,
They thought your death was the end.
They never dreamt you would rise again,
To forever take your kingly place.

Chorus
Jesus, Father God, Holy Spirit come and fill me,
Father, all I want to do is praise and worship you.

And even now after many years,
The life you give is still new.
And the light that shines from within our lives,
Will come only from your kingly place.

Chorus
Jesus, Father God, Holy Spirit come and fill me,
Spirit, all I want to do is praise and worship you.

END

I WANT TO SAY

I want to say to the mountain,
Mighty mountain move.
I want to say to the river,
Part and let me through.
I want to say to the ocean,
I am crossing you.
Because my Lord has told me to go.

Chorus
Lord when you tell me,
You empower me,
And you crown me, with your love.
Lord when you send me,
You defend me,
And you guide me, from above.

I want to say to my troubles,
Troubles let me go.
I want to say to the demons,
You're heading down below.
I want to say to temptation,
I have got control.
Because my Lord has told me to go.

Chorus

Lord let me say to the people,
God can set you free.
Lord let me say to your 'body',
You've got victory.
Lord let me say to your people,
Come and join with me.
Because our Lord has told us to go.

Chorus
END

MY PRAYER

I am a voice that's crying out,
"Make way for Christ the Lord."
But they won't hear, they wander lost,
And seek their own accord.
They care not for His grace and love,
They have their lust and power,
And in their sin they want to bathe,
Until their final hour.

O Father God, give my voice wings,
To cross the great divide,
To let them know the joy and peace,
The Spirit can provide.
Unblock their ears with words from You,
So they can hear the fire,
Unveil their eyes and let them see,
They're running to Your ire.

I'm just one voice, that stands alone.
A candle in the dark.
But You, oh Lord, can start a fire,
With just a single spark.
So Lord, from me, take all I am
And fill me with Your love.
Let all I say and do and think,
Flow from Your throne above.

Lord, let me lose my hopes and dreams,
To gain all that You are,
So my success is reaching souls,
through Your great grace and power.
Now I will kneel and give my gifts,
For You to work through me,
And watch, just like a passenger,
As prisoners are set free.

END

FEAR AND BELIEF

If I had seen,
Him hanging there broken,
Upon Calvary's tree,
Would I still believe?

If I had seen,
Him standing there nail scared,
Alive from the grave,
Would I still have fear?

'Cause I can know,
His marvellous scripture,
Which leads me to him,
I'll learn not to fear.

'Cause I have seen,
His wond'rous creation,
He made by his word,
I'll truly believe.

When I will rise,
To join him in heaven,
I'll stand at His throne,
And I'll have no fear.

Then he will say,
The words I have longed for,
Come home my sweet child,
For you have believed.

END

GOD'S BEST

I see the things that God has made.
I see the work of man.
There is no way man can compete,
With God's creating hand.
For at our best, all we can do,
Is build a shadow pale.
And at His worst, God's better than,
We ever can avail.

From all the stars and galaxies,
He placed to work as one,
To trees adorned with golden bloom,
Just shining like the sun.
All that God's hand and breath does touch,
Shouts out His holy name.
And when God comes to live in man,
Man never is the same.

So, when I'm told this earth is not,
God's final place for man,
My heart longs for that joyous day,
When He fulfils His plan.
Where His glory is full on show,
For all to see and feel.
So, let's all come and bow to Him,
So we can see it's real.

END

THRONE ROOM

The throne room opened before me,
In all its majesty.
With the elders all around Him,
God sat so quietly.

Yet there seemed a cloud of sadness,
Amid the glory's glow.
The depth of sadness touched me.
I felt the need to know.

So I humbly walked toward Him,
My Father on the throne,
And I felt His love surround me,
More than I'd ever known.

And yet, the sadness lingered,
As did the need to seek,
Then what I saw just shattered me,
Tears on my Father's cheek.

I ran to Him, with desperate need
And fell down at His feet.
"What is it, Lord?" I cried to Him,
As I felt two hearts meet.

He said, "My child, I wanted you,
To see this side of me.
To do the work I have for you,
It's this you need to see."

"Now all these tears are falling for,
The ones whose time has come.
In all the years I've given them,
They never loved my Son."

Continued next page…

"Although I gave them sun and rain
And beauty all around,
They never heard a word I said,
Their faith was earthly bound."

"Although I know not all will choose,
To love me and my Son,
My heart still breaks and tears fall,
With just the loss of one."

"And so, my child, you called to me,
To ask for work to do.
Now share my love to all you can,
Through gifts I've given you."

"Let people know my greatest joy,
Is when our hearts are one,
When hearts and heads are turned to me
And Jesus Christ my Son."

Then as His hand touched on my cheek,
I felt His love flow free,
And knew the message I'm to share,
For all eternity.

"All you're to do," He said to me,
"I open up the door,
And let my glory be released,
To touch the sick and poor."

"Now also know, my priceless child,
The task's not yours alone,
My Spirit goes to work through you,
To bring my children home."

END

SOMEONE

I'm all alone within this crowd,
My heart cries out to go.
There's Christians all around me here,
But none of them I know.

But God has called me to come here,
Though I still don't know why.
Surely, He hears my plea to leave.
Surely, He hears my cry.

Yet I still stand friendless and still,
Within the milling crowd.
"Lord lead me now or send me home,"
I almost cried aloud.

But God does not answer my call,
And I begin to doubt.
So I angle toward the door,
To give myself an out.

Beside the door I see someone,
With head turned to the ground,
And though there's no flashing of lights,
Or booming God-like sound,

I feel a gentle nudge within,
My heart to touch this soul.
"If this is you oh Mighty Lord,
I'll let you take control."

At first, I struggled with my words,
Not knowing what to say,
Until I thought I saw a smile
At something I did say.

Continued next page…

And then they started answering,
And we enjoyed the time.
Until with cake and coffee gone,
We promised one more time.

Then as Sunday came 'round once more,
To church I longed to go,
For I believed God led me there,
For someone I could know.

So, I thanked God for what He did,
As I went on my way,
And when I saw their face once more,
I felt joy fill my day.

But as we spoke, I felt there was,
Something they had to say.
So, in my fumbling way I asked,
If they were still okay.

Their answer shocked me to the core.
It made me see the light.
For they had planned to take their life,
Sometime last Sunday night.

But after they had talked with me,
They spent some hours in prayer.
Then they realised, to their relief,
That God does really care.

For they had been there several times,
And felt like cheese to chalk,
'Till God answered and gave someone,
who'd listen while they talk.

END

<u>TORN</u>

As time into the past does flow,
What is to come, we cannot know.
And as I age, I find I'm torn,
Between this world and Heaven's dawn.

Don't get me wrong, it's no contest,
There is no doubt, Heaven is best.
But I desire to let souls know,
They can escape the hell below.

So, 'though I yearn to rise above,
I also yearn to share God's love.
What comforts me and brings me rest,
Is God's in charge and He knows best.

END

IT'S TIME

Oh, don't you know, oh, don't you see,
It's not for you to look at me,
And see the one I used to be.

It's not for me to look at you,
And think of what you used to do,
It's time to let God's love shine through.

For Jesus came to take our past,
And time is moving way too fast,
For us to let the hurting last.

So, let it go, throw it away,
And in God's arms desire to stay,
For hurt will only make us stray.

As Heaven is our final goal,
Where God will love our hearts and soul,
Let's put ourselves in God's control.

And live right now, like we will then,
With love and grace our obsession,
And make this world just like Heaven.

END

LORD SHOW ME

Oh Lord show me what makes me stray,
What turns my heart and mind away.
What makes me step into the dark,
What makes me lose Your Spirit's spark.
It's Christ Jesus I want as Lord,
And with You, God, be in accord.

Lord show me what, within my heart,
I need to lose or make depart.
Help me to train my mind each day,
'Till I no longer want to stray.
Lord, day by day, help me to be,
Much more of You and less of me.

END

CAST THE FIRST STONE

At sunrise he appeared again,
Within the temple courts.
All the people gathered around,
Listening as he taught.
The teachers of the law came in,
With all the Pharisees.
They held a women's arms so tight,
Asking, Teacher hear us please.

We've caught this woman deep in sin,
Bedding another's man.
We're asking you her punishment,
Please tell us if you can.
The Law of Moses says we should,
Stone her right here and now.
What is to be her punishment,
Please Teacher, tell us now.

But Jesus in full patience turned,
And wrote upon the sand.
Then stopped their further questioning,
When he raised up his hand.
In wisdom he then placed them all,
Before the judgement throne.
Who truly is without a sin,
Casts the very first stone.

A silence fell upon the crowd,
As they recalled their sins.
Then turning they all walked away,
From all the woman sins.
"If none are left condemning you,
Then I condemn you not.
I love you and release you now,
Go leave your sinful lot."

END

HOW IS IT LORD

Of the billions upon this earth,
That lived and are to come,
How is it Lord, You know my name
And want to call me son?

With this world and the universe,
That You have to control,
How is it Lord, You wait for me,
To gently touch my soul?

With all the words and tears and cries,
Sent up to You each day,
How is it Lord, You know my needs,
Before I even pray?

With all the times I broke Your rules,
And pushed You far away,
How is it Lord, You love me so,
You shed Your blood that day?

END

TO SET ME FREE

Thank you, Jesus, for saving me,
You gave me love eternally.
You took my life so easily,
Then took my heart and set it free.

Thank you, Savoir, for loving me,
You gave your life so faithfully.
You cut the bonds that clung to me,
Then when I asked, you set me free.

Thank you, Master, for wanting me,
You loved me though I turned to flee.
You took me back so graciously,
Then in my need your love was free.

Thank you, Jesus, for telling me,
You took the cross so painfully.
You shed your blood to cover me,
Then gave your life to set me free.

END

SANCTIFY ME

I'll never be worthy, by the work of my hands,
To look at Your wonderful face.
I never could pay off, all the debt that I owe,
For room in Your Heavenly place.

But the price it was paid, by the blood of Your Son,
Shed up on that terrible tree.
I know I'm unworthy, for my failings and sin,
But always You sanctify me.

END

AS GREAT AS YOU

Remember now when Jesus said,
My time is soon to come.
Remember how on Calvary,
He said that it is done.
He gave his life so we may live,
A life that's cleansed of sin.
While we are waiting for that day,
When he will come again.

Remember Jesus promised us,
If we were true to him,
He'd stand beside us faithfully,
And wash us clean from sin.
Our praises to you Lord above,
We sing and sing so true.
We lift our voices and our hearts,
And offer them to you.

Lord Jesus hear our crying voice,
We sing to you as one.
We lift up high you holy name,
In praise till day is done.
And in our hearts there's none so great,
So faithful just and true.
For though great men have lived and died,
There's none as great as you.

In Jesus now I put my trust,
In him and him alone.
For without his true saving grace,
I never will go home.
Now in his hands I lay my life,
For him to make it new.
And when I die I'll see the land,
He's made for me and you.

END

LASTS ETERNITY

All I do is just like dust.
It crumbles and it fades.
Not one thing that I've made,
Lasts or is Heaven bade.

From You Lord, a single breath,
Will last eternity.
To my joy, You called my name,
And said that You want me.

END

JUST THE SAME

I can see with my own eyes,
And feel a tender touch.
When you strike with bitter lies,
My heart hurts just as much.

When I bruise it's black and blue,
And when I bleed its red.
When my life is lived all through,
Then I am just as dead.

Hidden deep within my heart,
Are yearnings not yet told.
Thoughts of songs and all the arts,
And ancient days of old.

Must I do what can't be done,
To make you understand?
Must I fall my world undone,
For you to lend a hand?

When it's all been said and done,
And judgement must be made.
We are both to face the Son,
Then go the way we're bade.

Though some say I am 'broken',
And 'normal' can't be mine.
Praise the Lord I'm going home,
When Jesus says it's time.

END

<u>BEYOND</u>

Oh death, where is your sting,
For those rebirth has claimed?
They sing toward the skies,
For they all know they're named.

All those in Book of Life,
No more are in your count.
For they are washed in blood,
They've drunk from Holy Fount'.

They're eyes all look beyond,
Where new lives last for e're.
Where your arms ne'er can reach,
Where they breathe Heaven's air.

END

IN THE GLORY

What wonders do abound,
In glory of my Lord.
There is no greater sound,
Then hearing from You, God.

When heart and mind do see,
What only God can give.
Then man's desires do flee,
As souls cry out to live.

When faith accepts your grace,
That frees the prisoner bound.
Your Spirit takes its place,
To seal the new life found.

From earthly gods we turn,
To give you all control.
And love you we do yearn,
With heart and mind and soul.

'Till trump makes final call,
To judgment throne above.
When sheep will answer call,
To endless time of love.

END

FROM THE GRAVE

Good tidings my fellows,
Good tidings with love.
Good tiding from Jesus,
My Lord up above.

He suffered so greatly,
But cried out for peace.
Though none would befall him,
The pain would not cease.

He cried out, "Its finished,"
The job had been done.
It was a long battle,
But Jesus had won.

He gave up his life then,
To die on the cross.
So we may not suffer,
That terrible loss.

Continued next page…

The priests judged him guilty,
The crowd had him tried.
They thought it was over,
They watched as he died.

They carried his body,
To lay in a tomb.
They rolled in a bolder,
To seal up his doom.

He came back unbroken,
Came back from the grave.
Then they knew he died there,
Just so he could save.

He can give us freedom,
He can give us love.
And He'll cut what's binding,
From life up above.

END

COMMUNION THING

Hello Jesus, it's me again,
I hope that you remember me.
When I came here a week ago,
They said that you would set me free.

Remember them, the Christian folk,
They had that strange Communion thing.
They ate some bread and drank some wine,
And then they all stood up to sing.

What it all meant I didn't know,
So I just sat there in the pew.
And waited 'till the song was sung,
I didn't know what I should do.

Since then we've talked both you and I,
About the cross and Calvary.
And you showed me, where in God's word,
It says that you had died for me.

It took some time to just sink in,
Into this great thick skull of mine.
And two more days to reach my heart,
But you made it happen in time.

Continued next page...

And now I know what each part means,
Within this great Communion thing.
And though I know I've much to learn,
I understand now why I'll sing.

For every time I eat some bread,
I am reminded that you died.
And 'cause you died to take my sin,
I feel so free deep down inside.

And every time I drink some wine,
I almost feel your cleansing blood.
That washes all the sins away,
Which stuck to me like gooey mud.

So, Jesus, Lord, each Sunday morn,
When Communion I always take.
I'll eat and drink and sing as well,
Because you died for my own sake.

END

Until we meet, or meet again –

May the grace of the Lord Jesus Christ, the love of God, and the fellowship of the Holy Spirit be with you all. (2 Corinthians 13:14)

Rod Loader